vickie howell

knit aid

A Learn It, Fix It, Finish It Guide
for Knitters on the Go

STERLING

New York / London
www.sterlingpublishing.com

Library of Congress Cataloging-in-Publication Data

Howell, Vickie.
  Knit aid : a learn it, fix it, finish it guide for knitters on the go / Vickie Howell.
      p. cm.
  Includes index.
  ISBN-13: 978-1-4027-4681-9
  ISBN-10: 1-4027-4681-4
  1. Knitting. I. Title.

TT820H813145 2007
746.43'2041—dc22

2006100966

10   9   8   7   6   5   4   3   2   1

Published by Sterling Publishing Co., Inc.
387 Park Avenue South, New York, NY 10016
©2008 by Vickie Howell
Distributed in Canada by Sterling Publishing
C/o Canadian Manda Group, 165 Dufferin Street
Toronto, Ontario, Canada M6K 3H6
Distributed in the United Kingdom by GMC Distribution Services,
Castle Place, 166 High Street, Lewes, East Sussex, England BN7 1XU
Distributed in Australia by Capricorn Link (Australia) Pty. Ltd.
P.O. Box 704, Windsor, NSW 2756, Australia

BOOK DESIGN AND LAYOUT: Margo Mooney
ILLUSTRATIONS: Leela Corman

Printed in China

Sterling ISBN-13: 978-1-4027-4681-9
       ISBN-10: 1-4027-4681-4

For information about custom editions, special sales, premium and
corporate purchases, please contact Sterling Special Sales
Department at 800-805-5489 or specialsales@sterlingpublishing.com.

To Tammy Izbicki
and Dave Campbell,
my Libra bookends,
whose support keeps
my sarcasm in
check and my sanity
in existence.

contents

preface

From the minute I started knitting, it was love at first stitch. Something about the endless possibilities of color, texture, and outcome combined with the benefit of portability, screamed creative perfection to me. Even before it was something I did professionally, knitting consumed much of my time. When I wasn't actually knitting, I still wanted to hear about it, read about it, talk about it, and hang out with others who felt the same. To this day, I'm one of those hopelessly devoted Knitties who's never without a project (or five). Because my life tends to be a little on the hectic side and I'm often on the go, I have to take my knitting time where I can get it. Yeah, that's me, the quirky gal, needles clicking away in line at the grocery store, in the middle of dinner parties, in the passenger seat of the car, during meetings, or at the sidelines of one of my sons' extracurricular activities. It would not surprise me if people thought it strange the way that I incorporate craftiness into daily life, but what I'm finding out is quite the opposite. Today's knitter doesn't necessarily have the luxury of lounging around for hours on end knitting her or himself into a fiber-y coma (although if you happen to be lucky enough to fit into that category, I bow in envy before you). The craziness of modern life demands creativity not only within our knitting patterns, but also in fitting the knitting of them into our schedules. So, this book is for you, the knitter on the go who may occasionally need pocket-sized knowledge at the ready, and in a pinch. After all, everybody can use a little help sometimes, and *Knit Aid* promises to be there when you do.

Knit on!

goodwill embassknitter

QUICK TIPS

Tips For New Knitters

1. Find a yarn and project you're excited about. The more you love the tools you're working with, the more likely you are to stick with your knitting.

2. Get a book. Whether it's this one that you can easily throw in your knitting bag, or a larger reference book to keep at home, find a written how-to helper that works for you!

3. Go online. There are a lot of great photo and video tutorials you can watch for free on the Web. These are especially awesome when you're stuck on a project late at night; help at your fingertips without having to change out of your jammies. That, my friends, is good stuff!

4. Ask for help. If you're lucky enough to have someone close to you who knits, then by all means, enlist their knitting expertise. If you don't, head over to your local yarn shop and ask one of the employees. Trust me; they want to answer your questions. The better a knitter you become, the more likely you are to buy tons of stuff from their store!

5. Join a group. So much of knitting is about community—what you're putting out as well as what you can get back—and knitting groups are not only great social outlets, but an invaluable meeting of minds. Whether you've never knit a stitch before or you're a full blown knitster, there's always something to learn from a group of fellow stitch 'n bitchers!

Tips for Busy Knitters

1. If you're really short on time, be realistic with your project choices. Pick something quick and easy to knit so you don't get frustrated by lack of progress.

2. Whether it's English or Continental, choose the method of knitting that proves speediest for you.

3. In general, slick, lightweight metal needles and clean (non-novelty) fibers are quickest to knit with. The stitches glide off of the needles nicely and it's easier to catch mistakes when there aren't extraneous yarn bits masking your knittin' and purlin'.

4. Keep a small project in your bag or car so when you find yourself waiting around in line at the DMV or sitting at the doctor's office, you can use that time to knit. After all, craftiness is the best cure for the irritation one is sure to feel during life's time-sucking obligations.

5. If you've got kids, bring your project to your child's soccer practice, dance rehearsal, or art class, and knit from the sidelines.

6. TV time is knitting time! Every time you pop a movie into the DVD player or click "play" on that Tivo, pick up your needles. Multi-tasking = good.

7. If you carpool or ride public transportation to work, bring your knitting along. Knitting in places like the subway is a great way to pass the time!

8. Add knitting to your calendar. If you make craftiness part of your daily, weekly, or monthly routine, then you'll be more likely to stick with it.

9. Teach your friends and family to knit. This way you can combine quality bonding time with knitting time!

10. Knit in bed. Although your partner may not be thrilled with this suggestion, knitting while watching a little nighttime TV is a great way to wind down from a busy day.

abbreviations

K	knit		**cont**	continue, continuing
P	purl		**dpn(s)**	double-pointed needle(s)
CO	cast on		**RH**	right hand
BO	bind off		**LH**	left hand
St st	stockinette stitch (alternate between knit and purl rows)		**RS**	right side
			WS	wrong side
St (s)	stitch(es)		**pat**	pattern
YO	yarn over		**rem**	remaining
dec	decrease		**rep**	repeat
inc	increase		**pm**	place marker
M1	make one stitch		**sl**	slip
K2tog	knit two stitches together		**PSSO**	pass slipped stitch over
K2togtbl	knit 2 stitches together through back loop		**tbl**	through the back loop
ssk	slip, slip, knit (slip 2 stitches knitwise, one at a time, then knit them together through the back loop)		**SKPO**	slip 1 st, knit 1 st, pass slipped st over knit st
			S2KPO	slip 2 sts together, knit 1, pass 2 slipped sts over.
rnd	round		**2YO**	double yarnover (= 2 sts on next row)
MC	main color		**ch**	chain
CC	contrasting color		**sc**	single crochet
approx	approximately		**p2tog**	purl 2 together
beg	beginning			

k f & b	knit into front and back		*** or ****	starting (and ending) point to repeat instructions
rem	remaining		**rep from ***	repeat all the instructions following the asterisk
sl	slip			
sl-w-t	slip, wrap, turn			
wyib	with yarn in back		**work even**	work in pattern without increasing or decreasing any stitches
wyif	with yarn in front			
dc	double crochet			
hdc	half-double crochet		**working yarn**	strand coming from ball, i.e., not the tail

Web/Blog Abbreviations

Time spent typing about knitting is less time spent actually knitting. That just will not do, so a whole new slew of abbreviations can be used when chatting with your virtual knitting peeps. After all, a second saved is a stitch-ish earned!

FO	Finished Object		**HTH**	Hope this helps
UFO	Unfinished Object		**HK!**	Happy Knitting!
WIP	Work in Progress		**VK**	*Vogue Knitting*
KIP	Knit in Public		**IK**	*Interweave Knits*
KAL	Knit Along		**FCEK**	*Family Circle Easy Knitting*
Tink	Unknit (knit spelled backwards)			
			K.1	*Knit.1 Magazine*
TIA	Thanks in advance		**OTK**	on the needles
OT	off topic		**LYS**	Local Yarn Store
OKC	Obligatory Knitting Content			

first aid knit

TOOLS FOR YOUR OWN KNIT KIT

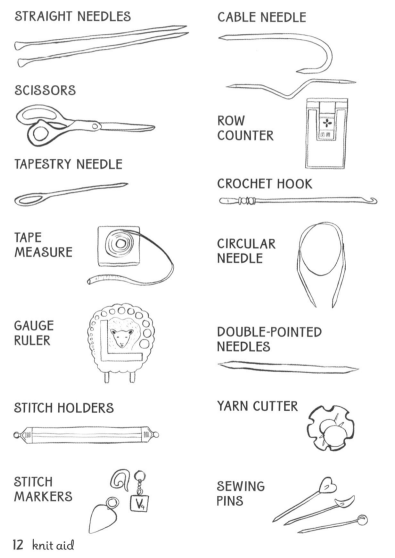

STRAIGHT NEEDLES

SCISSORS

TAPESTRY NEEDLE

TAPE MEASURE

GAUGE RULER

STITCH HOLDERS

STITCH MARKERS

CABLE NEEDLE

ROW COUNTER

CROCHET HOOK

CIRCULAR NEEDLE

DOUBLE-POINTED NEEDLES

YARN CUTTER

SEWING PINS

YARN WEIGHTS

E ven very different fibers like smooth wool and furry acrylic can have a common characteristic: weight. Since weights can directly translate into gauge, it's helpful to know what you're looking for by yarn type.

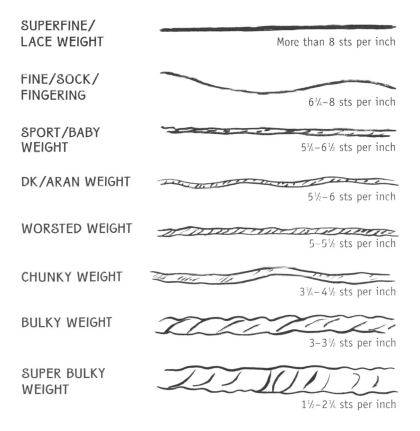

SUPERFINE/ LACE WEIGHT

More than 8 sts per inch

FINE/SOCK/ FINGERING

6¾–8 sts per inch

SPORT/BABY WEIGHT

5¾–6½ sts per inch

DK/ARAN WEIGHT

5½–6 sts per inch

WORSTED WEIGHT

5–5½ sts per inch

CHUNKY WEIGHT

3¾–4½ sts per inch

BULKY WEIGHT

3–3½ sts per inch

SUPER BULKY WEIGHT

1½–2¾ sts per inch

needle exchange

THE SCOOP ON KNITTING NEEDLES

You have several different choices available when it comes to knitting needles. For the most part it doesn't really matter which you go with since technically, they'll all get the job done. What does matter though, is that you pick needles you enjoy working with. Just like finding the right yarn, needles can make or break your knitting adventure. That's right, I said knitting "adventure" (to be said, using "jazz hands")! Here are your options:

Aluminum

Aluminum needles are super inexpensive and available at all craft stores. These are my least favorite of the bunch, but if I had to choose between using them and not knitting at all, it would be no contest. I don't recommend using aluminum when working with slick yarns—this combo makes it difficult to keep the stitches on the needles—but other than that, they work just fine. Oh, and bonus: they've got an old-school nostalgia about them and make a cool, almost sword-like "ching-ching" sound when they slide against each other!

Plastic

Another affordable, accessible option. Plastic needles are flexible, light-weight, and available in a ton of cool colors.

Resin

Fairly new to the market, these are the lightest weight needles I've ever worked with. I absolutely love knitting with resin needles (best-known brand is currently Crystal Palace's "Daisy" Needles) not only because they're gentle on the wrists and manipulate the yarn easily, but also at under $10 a pair, they won't break the bank! Their only downfall is they're not as accessible as their plastic sisters; they're only available online and in select yarn shops.

Wood

Wood needles are lovely, warming, and wonderful to work with. Unfortunately however, the nicest versions can be quite pricey. I recommend treating yourself to a pair in a size you use frequently, but then going with a more affordable option for the bulk of your collection. Money saved on needles = more money to spend on yarn!

Bamboo

Oh bamboo, how I ♥ you! Available at most major craft stores and reasonably priced, these babies are damn near needle perfection. They're lightweight, flexible, and warm in your hands. Although some knitters prefer not to use bamboo (or wooden) needles when working with high-traction yarns like wool, I find that overall, bamboo can R-O-C-K any project!

Nickel-plated Brass

You'll feel like a superhero knitting with these needles. Designed for speed and ease, your yarn will fly off of these shining beauties! If you can afford to shell out the cash, I highly recommend using these (most common brand is Addi Turbo circulars) whenever you're working with any non-slick fiber. Seriously people, it's like knitting with a Cadillac. Wait, what? Well, you know what I mean.

band-aid

READING A BALL BAND

DESIGNATES WEIGHT CLASS OF YARN.
1 = super fine, 2 = fine, 3 = light,
4 = medium, 5 = bulky, 6 = super bulky

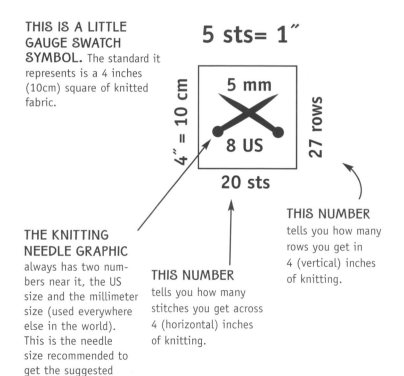

THIS IS A LITTLE GAUGE SWATCH SYMBOL. The standard it represents is a 4 inches (10cm) square of knitted fabric.

5 sts= 1″

4″ = 10 cm

5 mm

8 US

27 rows

20 sts

THE KNITTING NEEDLE GRAPHIC always has two numbers near it, the US size and the millimeter size (used everywhere else in the world). This is the needle size recommended to get the suggested gauge.

THIS NUMBER tells you how many stitches you get across 4 (horizontal) inches of knitting.

THIS NUMBER tells you how many rows you get in 4 (vertical) inches of knitting.

MACHINE WASH OK, AT THE TEMPERATURE NOTED.

OK TO DRY CLEAN, ANY SOLVENT

DO NOT IRON

HAND WASH ONLY

OK TO USE IRON ON LOW SETTING

DRY FLAT

OK TO USE IRON ON MEDIUM SETTING

DO NOT WASH

DO NOT BLEACH

OK TO USE IRON ON HIGH SETTING

BLEACHING PERMITTED (WITH CHLORINE)

DO NOT TUMBLE DRY

DO NOT DRY CLEAN

winds of change

WINDING YARN

Winding a Center-Pull Ball

1. Let a 4-6 inches tail hang loosely (or secure it with your pinky and ring finger), while wrapping the yarn around your thumb and pointer finger, figure-8 style. Wrap 15 or so more times.

2. Slide the yarn off your fingers and pinch it into a wad, placing your thumb over the tail.

3. Wind the yarn around and around the wad, going different ways crosswise, but taking care to keep thumb over tail so you don't wind over it. Keep on keepin' on until yarn is completely wound. Oh, and it's totally no big deal if you do accidentally cover up the tail. In that case you won't have a center-pull ball, but a ball you can knit from nonetheless!

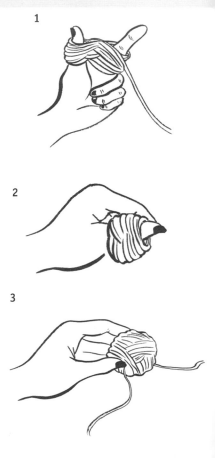

1

2

3

HOW IT ALL UNWINDS

HANK Often higher-end yarn is sold in loosely wrapped hanks to allow the fiber to breathe while being stored. You can't, however, knit directly from a hank without turning it into a great, big ol' tangled mess. Before you start your new project, make sure to wind it into a ball or cake first!

SKEIN Most common way that craft yarn is wound.

BALL What you get when you wind by hand.

CAKE The result when you wind the yarn using a fancy-schmancy ball winder.

schematics

A schematic is essentially a pattern's blueprint. It's a great visual tool, showing the general shape and measurements of a project.

These numbers show the width and length in inches of one piece. The number preceding the parenthesis is for the smallest size, the numbers inside the parentheses are for the other sizes
(getting larger from left to right).

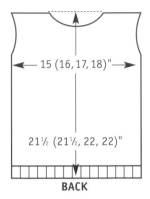

←— 15 (16, 17, 18)"—→

21½ (21½, 22, 22)"

BACK

knit note

>> Remember, when the numbers on a schematic are for something wearable, they won't necessarily be the same as your own measurements. It'll all depend on how you want the garment to fit. The difference between your body measurements and the piece's measurements is known as *ease*. Here are some measurement guidelines to help you out.

FIT	BODY MEASUREMENT PLUS X INCHES
Super tight	0"
Tight	1–2"
Standard	2–4"
Loose	4–6"
Super loose	6–8"

that's about the size of knit!

STANDARD GARMENT SIZING

For Wee Ones

Baby's Size (months)	3	6	12	18	24
1. Chest (in.)	16	17	18	19	20
(cm)	*40.5*	*43*	*45.4*	*48*	*50.5*
2. Center Back Neck-to-Cuff	$10^{1}/_{2}$	$11^{1}/_{2}$	$12^{1}/_{2}$	14	18
	26.5	*29*	*31.5*	*35.5*	*45.5*
3. Back Waist Length	6	7	$7^{1}/_{2}$	8	$8^{1}/_{2}$
	15.5	*17.5*	*19*	*20.5*	*21.5*
4. Cross Back (shoulder to shoulder)	$7^{1}/_{4}$	$7^{3}/_{4}$	$8^{1}/_{4}$	$8^{1}/_{2}$	$8^{3}/_{4}$
	18.5	*19.5*	*21*	*21.5*	*22*
5. Sleeve Length to Underarm	6	$6^{1}/_{2}$	$7^{1}/_{2}$	8	$8^{1}/_{2}$
	15.5	*16.5*	*19*	*20.5*	*21.5*

Reprinted by permission from *STANDARDS & GUIDELINES FOR CROCHET AND KNITTING*, (Craft Yarn Council of America, 2005).

STANDARD GARMENT SIZING

For Children

Child's size	2	4	6	8	10
1. Chest (in.)	21	23	25	$26^1/_2$	28
(cm.)	*53*	*58.5*	*63.5*	*67*	*71*
2. Center Back Neck-to-Cuff	18	$19^1/_2$	$20^1/_2$	22	24
	45.5	*49.5*	*52*	*56*	*61*
3. Back Waist Length	$8^1/_2$	$9^1/_2$	$10^1/_2$	$12^1/_2$	14
	21.5	*24*	*26.5*	*31.5*	*35.5*
4. Cross Back (Shoulder to shoulder)	$9^1/_4$	$9^3/_4$	$10^1/_4$	$10^3/_4$	$11^1/_4$
	23.5	*25*	*26*	*27*	*28.5*
5. Sleeve Length to Underarm	$8^1/_2$	$10^1/_2$	$11^1/_2$	$12^1/_2$	$13^1/_2$
	21.5	*26.5*	*29*	*31.5*	*34.5*

Child's (cont.)	12	14	16
1. Chest (in.)	30	$31^1/_2$	$32^1/_2$
(cm.)	*76*	*80*	*82.5*
2. Center Back Neck-to-Cuff	26	27	28
	66	*68.5*	*71*
3. Back Waist Length	15	$15^1/_2$	16
	38	*39.5*	*40.5*
4. Cross Back (Shoulder to shoulder)	12	$12^1/_4$	13
	30.5	*31*	*33*
5. Sleeve Length to Underarm	15	16	$16^1/_2$
	38	*40.5*	*42*

Reprinted by permission from *STANDARDS & GUIDELINES FOR CROCHET AND KNITTING,* (Craft Yarn Council of America, 2005).

STANDARD GARMENT SIZING

For Women

Woman's Size	X-Small	Small	Medium	Large	
1. Bust (in.)	28–30	32–34	36–38	40–42	
(cm.)	*71–76*	*81–86*	*91.5–96.5*	*101.5–106.5*	
2. Center Back Neck-to-Cuff	27–27 1/2	28–28 1/2	29–29 1/2	30–30 1/2	
	68.5–70	*71–72.5*	*73.5–75*	*76–77.5*	
3. Back Waist Length	16 1/2	17	17 1/4	17 1/2	
	42	*43*	*43.5*	*44.5*	
4. Cross Back (Shoulder to shoulder)	14–14 1/2	14 1/2–15	16–16 1/2	17–17 1/2	
	35.5–37	*37–38*	*40.5–42*	*43–44.5*	
5. Sleeve Length to Underarm	16 1/2	17	17	17 1/2	
	42	*43*	*43*	*44.5*	

Woman's (cont.)	1x	2x	3x	4x	5x
1. Bust (in.)	44–46	48–50	52–54	56–58	60–62
(cm.)	*111.5–117*	*122–127*	*132–137*	*142–147*	*152–158*
2. Center Back Neck-to-Cuff	31–31 1/2	31 1/2–32	32 1/2–33	32 1/2–33	33–33 1/2
	78.5–80	*80–81.5*	*82.5–84*	*82.5–84*	*84–85*
3. Back Waist Length	17 3/4	18	18	18 1/2	18 1/2
	45	*45.5*	*45.5*	*47*	*47*
4. Cross Back (Shoulder to shoulder)	17 1/2	18	18	18 1/2	18 1/2
	44.5	*45.5*	*45.5*	*47*	*47*
5. Sleeve Length to Underarm	17 1/2	18	18	18 1/2	18 1/2
	44.5	*45.5*	*45.5*	*47*	*47*

Reprinted by permission from *STANDARDS & GUIDELINES FOR CROCHET AND KNITTING*, (Craft Yarn Council of America, 2005).

STANDARD GARMENT SIZING

For Men

Man's Size	Small	Medium	Large	X-Large	XX-Large
1. Chest (in.)	34–36	38–40	42–44	46–48	50–52
(cm.)	*86–91.5*	*96.5–101.5*	*106.5–111.5*	*116.5–122*	*127–132*
2. Center Back	32–32$^1/_2$	33–33$^1/_2$	34–34$^1/_2$	35–35$^1/_2$	36–36$^1/_2$
Neck-to-Cuff	*81–82.5*	*83.5–85*	*86.5–87.5*	*89–90*	*91.5–92.5*
3. Back Hip	25–25$^1/_2$	26$^1/_2$–26$^3/_4$	27–27$^1/_4$	27$^1/_2$–27$^3/_4$	28–28$^1/_2$
Length	*63.5–64.5*	*67.5–68*	*68.5–69*	*69.5–70.5*	*71–72.5*
4. Cross Back	15$^1/_2$–16	16$^1/_2$–17	17$^1/_2$–18	18–18$^1/_2$	18$^1/_2$–19
(Shoulder	*39.5–40.5*	*42–43*	*44.5–45.5*	*45.5–47*	*47–48*
to shoulder)					
5. Sleeve Length	18	18$^1/_2$	19$^1/_2$	20	20$^1/_2$
to Underarm	*45.5*	*47*	*49.5*	*50.5*	*52*

Reprinted by permission from *STANDARDS & GUIDELINES FOR CROCHET AND KNITTING,* (Craft Yarn Council of America, 2005).

STANDARD GARMENT SIZING

Head Circumference Chart

Infant/Child

	PREMIE	BABY
in.	12	14
cm.	30.5	35.5

	TODDLER	CHILD
in.	16	18
cm.	40.5	45.5

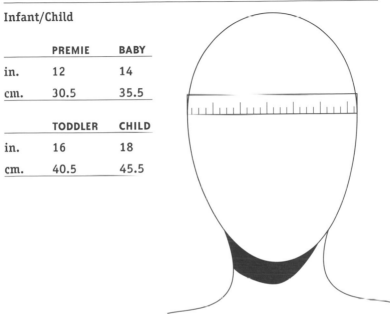

Reprinted by permission from *STANDARDS & GUIDELINES FOR CROCHET AND KNITTING*, (Craft Yarn Council of America, 2005).

slipknots and casting on

There are several different ways to cast stitches onto a needle. Often, the choice is only a matter of preference, so unless the project calls for a particular method, pick one you dig and get knitty with it!

Slipknot

This is the basic knot you may've learned in Scouts as a kid. It's often used in knitting and crochet to cast on the first stitch of a project.

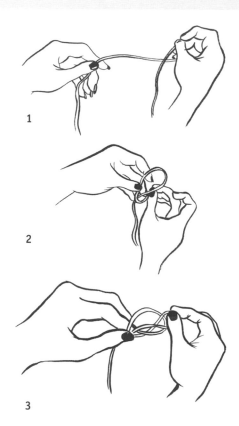

1. Leaving a tail, make a cursive "e"-looking loop with the yarn.

2. Holding onto the area where the yarn crosses with one hand, use the other hand to push a new loop through the existing loop.

3. Pull the loop and the two hanging strands snuggly until your slipknot is formed and slip it onto the needle.

"E"- Cast-On

By far the easiest of methods, it can be used to cast on stitches mid-row and is a great option when teaching young kids. The "E"-Cast-On does not, however, provide a nice finished edge. For that reason, it may not be the best choice for pieces without a knit or crocheted edging added or those requiring later seaming.

With your right hand (OK to reverse whole process if left-handed) hold a 4-6 inches tail with your pinky and ring finger.

1. Wrapping the working yarn around your thumb, make what looks like a cursive "e".

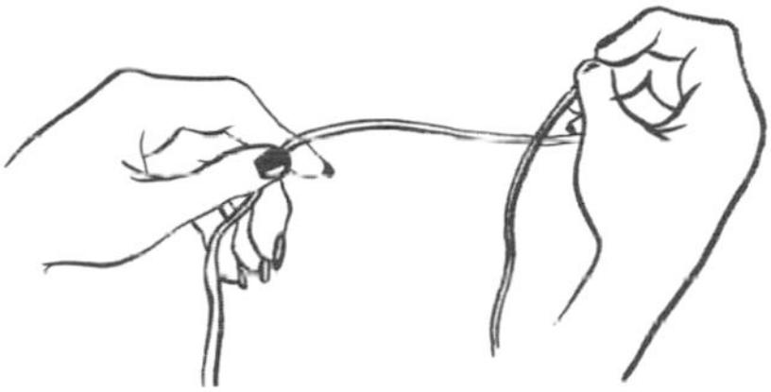

2. With a knitting needle in your right hand, bring the needle up through the loop on your thumb.

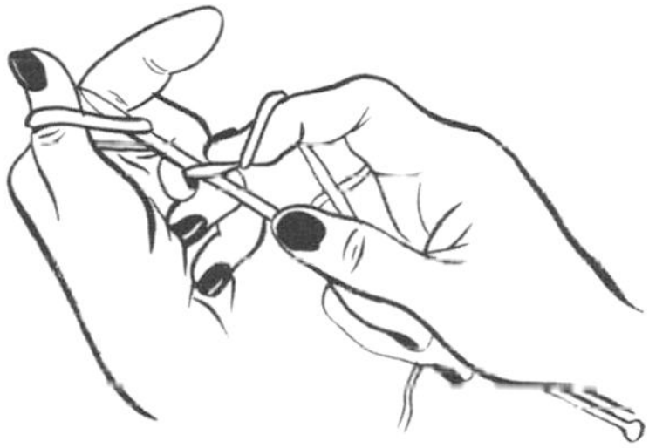

3. Remove your thumb while simultaneously pulling the working yarn so the stitch is secured (but not too tight) on the needle.

Once the first stitch is cast on, you can forget about holding onto the yarn tail.

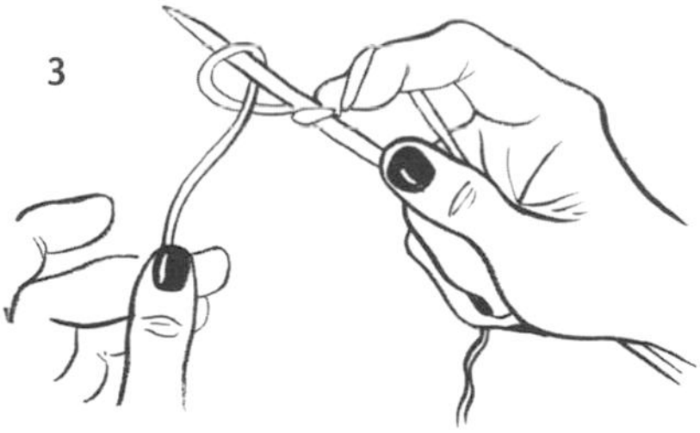

4. (Optional) Simply continue wrapping yarn and place the loop on the needle as seen above.

Repeat for as many stitches as the project requires.

Single Cast-On

When I re-learned to knit, I was taught this method by a well-known store owner. For some reason students seem to have a harder time wrapping their minds around this one at first, but once it clicks, it makes for a great, super-versatile cast-on!

You'll need about an inch of yarn for each stitch that you'll be casting on; this will be your tail.

1. Hold tail securely with your pinky and ring finger and wrap the working yarn around your thumb clockwise, letting it hang. You'll now see a backwards, cursive, "e"-looking loop around your thumb.

2. Come up through the bottom of the loop with a knitting needle.

3. Holding the needle between your thumb and forefinger, wrap the working yarn around the needle counterclockwise.

4. Transfer the loop from your thumb onto the needle by dipping the needle into the loop and scooping it off.

Repeat until you have cast on the desired number of stitches.

knit Rx

KNOTTY NURSE

The first stitch may seem a little persnickety. If it gives you any trouble, start with a slipknot and then proceed.

Knitted Cast-On

My mom uses this one! It's a great, all-purpose cast-on for anyone who knows the knit stitch.

1. Leaving a 4-6 inches tail, place a slipknot (see page 26) onto the left-hand needle. This acts as your first cast-on stitch.

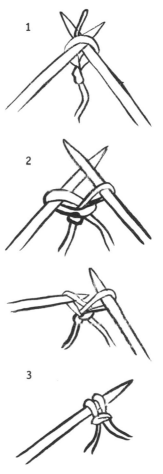

2. Knit (see page 33) into the stitch, but instead of pulling the old loop off of the left-hand needle, keep it there.

3. Then slip the new loop (stitch) back onto the left-hand needle as well.

Repeat until you have cast on the desired number of stitches.

Double Cast-On (a.k.a. Long-Tail Cast-On)

This method seems the most popular among the newest generation of knitters. It not only casts the yarn onto the needle, but also creates your first row of knitting.

Just as with the Single Cast-On (see pg 28), allow about an inch of yarn for each stitch you'll be casting on; this will be your tail.

1. Letting the tail hang, tie a slipknot around one of your knitting needles. You'll now have two strands of yarn hanging down from your needle (the tail, and the strand connected to the ball).

2. Take the needle in your right hand, and with your thumb and pointer finger on your left hand, separate the two strands of yarn.

3. Secure both loose ends under your ring finger and pinky (if you pull the needle down towards your palm, you'll see that loops have formed around both fingers).

4. Take your needle and scoop **under** the outer strand of the thumb loop . . .

5. Then **over** the inner strand of the pointer finger loop. Let the loop fall off your thumb and pull the tail so the stitch fits loosely onto the needle.

Repeat until you have cast on the desired number of stitches.

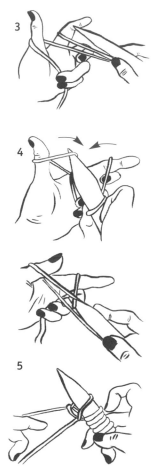

Cable Cast-on

This method gives a more elastic edge than other methods. It's particularly great for casting on extra stitches in the middle of a project!

This cast-on requires that you already have at least two stitches on your needle to begin. If you're using this method to start a project, follow the steps for the Knitted Cast-On (page 29) to establish the first two stitches. From there, you're ready to begin!

1. Insert the right-hand needle into the space between the last two (or possibly only two, if you're just getting started) stitches.

2. Wrap yarn counterclockwise around the right-hand needle.

3. Pull the loop through the space.

4. Slip this new stitch onto the left-hand needle.

Repeat until you have cast on the desired number of stitches.

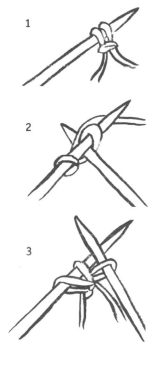

knit Rx

LOOSEN UP

If you find you are casting on too tightly, making your first row "H-E-Double Hockey Sticks" to knit, use a needle a size or two larger when you cast on. Once you're ready to start knitting switch back to the original needle.

double-stranding from the same ball

If a project calls for double-stranding, but doesn't require the yardage of more than one ball, simply pull a strand from both the beginning and the end of the ball, holding them together as if one strand of yarn. Knit as usual.

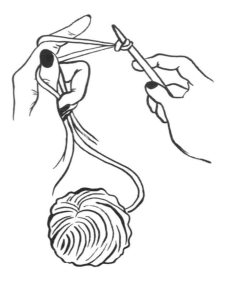

Joining a New Ball or Color

A new ball of yarn should only generally be joined at the beginning of a row. Otherwise, you risk the possibility of a big ol' hole in your project.

When you're ready to join another ball of yarn:

1. Drop the "old" working yarn and begin knitting with the "new" working yarn. (1) I find that it's helpful to knit a stitch or two

2. And then go back and loosely tie the two tails of yarn together (2) to keep it all secure. Once you've finished your project, untie all knots and weave in the ends.

florence knitengale

THE KNIT STITCH

English Method

Hold the needle with the stitches in your left hand. For the knit stitch worked the English way, the working yarn is held in your *right* hand and in the back of the work.

1. Insert your right-hand needle from bottom to top, into the stitch (the tips of your needles will form an "X").

2. Use your *right* index finger to wrap the strand of yarn (in a counterclockwise motion) around the right-hand needle.

3. Bring yarn through the stitch with right-hand needle . . .

4. And then pull the loop off the left-hand needle. You now have one complete knit stitch on your right-hand needle. Continue until the end of the row or as pattern directs.

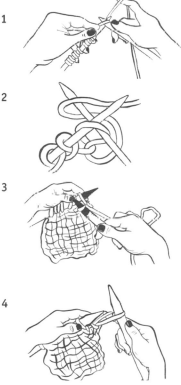

1

2

3

4

Continental Method

Hold the needle with the stitches in your left hand. For the knit stitch worked the Continental way, the working yarn is held in your *left* hand and in back of the work.

1. Insert the right-hand needle from bottom to top, into the stitch (the tips of your needles will form an "X").

2. Use your *left* index finger to wrap the strand of yarn (in a counterclockwise motion) around the right-hand needle.

3. Bring the yarn through the stitch with the right-hand needle . . .

4. And then pull the loop off the left-hand needle. You now have one complete knit stitch on your right-hand needle. Continue until the end of the row or as pattern directs.

knit ℞

PRACTICE MAKES PERFKNIT!

Easy Knit Stitch Scarf A great way to practice your knit stitch is by making a cool, but simple garter stitch scarf.

Using a chunky weight yarn, CO 24 sts. Knit every row until scarf measures as long as you are tall (or desired length). BO. Weave in ends.

we are the purled

THE PURL STITCH

English Method

Hold the needle with the stitches in your left hand. For the purl stitch worked the English way, the working yarn is held in the *right* hand and in front of the work.

1. Insert the right-hand needle from top to bottom into the stitch.

2. Use your *right* index finger to wrap the strand of yarn (in a counter-clockwise motion) around the right-hand needle.

3. Bring the yarn through the stitch with the right-hand needle . . .

4. And then pull loop off the left-hand needle. Continue until the end of the row or as pattern directs.

1

2

3

Continental Method

Hold the needle with the stitches in your left hand. For the purl stitch worked the Continental way, the working yarn is held in the *left* hand and in the front of the work.

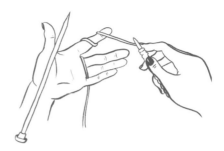

1. Insert your right-hand needle from top to bottom, into the stitch.

2. Use your *left* index finger to wrap the strand of yarn (in a counterclockwise motion) around the right-hand needle.

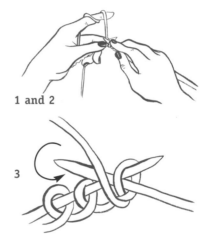

1 and 2

3

3. Use the tip of the right-hand needle to scoop the yarn, bringing it through the stitch while pulling the loop off the left-hand needle. Continue until the end of the row or as pattern directs.

recognizing stitches

K nowing how to decipher a knit stitch from a purl stitch is the first step towards keeping track of where you are in your work. Whether you're working in stockinette, ribbing, or seed stitch, if you can tell which stitch you did last then you'll always know what comes next!

The knit stitch looks like a "V." This is the "right" or public side of a stockinette stitch piece.

The purl stitch looks like a little bump. This is the "wrong" or non-public side of a stockinette stitch piece.

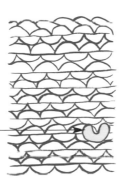

AKNITOMY OF A STITCH

KNIT 411 Knitting is a series of overlapping loops. If you were to look at a single, isolated knit stitch, it would look sort of like an upside down rain drop. The bumps you see on the "wrong" side of a stockinette stitch piece are simply the curved tops of the rain drop folded down over each other.

picking up stitches

Picking up stitches may be required for any number of reasons including adding a neckline, embellishing edges, or changing the direction of your knitting.

If you're picking up stitches along a bound-off edge, insert your needle into the space under both loops of the existing stitch. Lay the yarn over the needle and scoop it through the hole. (Can be 1 drawing with arrow) You'll now have one stitch on the needle.

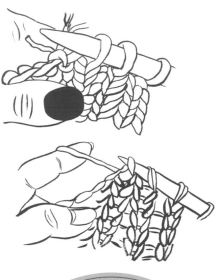

*Insert the needle into the next space, wrap the yarn counterclockwise, and scoop the loop through the space. Repeat from * until you have picked up the desired number of stitches.

knit note

>> If you're working with a garter stitch piece (knitting every row), just pick up stitches between the ridge bumps.

knit ℞

DIVIDE AND CONQUER

To make sure that picked-up stitches along a curved neck or shoulder line are distributed evenly, divide the area into quarters and mark each section with a pin. Then, pick up ¼ of the desired stitches in each section and you'll be smooth sailin'!

tension relief—gauge

C hecking your gauge is the most important skill you need to produce knitted items with accurate sizing. Gauge (a.k.a. tension) is simply the number of rows and stitches there are per knitted inch. This number will vary depending on the yarn weight, needle size, and your personal knitting tension.

To determine gauge, knit a 4-inch (although I often cheat and knit less and it's usually fine) swatch, lay it flat, and using either a tape measure or handy dandy gauge ruler, measure one inch's worth of stitches both horizontally (stitches) and vertically (rows).

Often a pattern will list gauge based on a 4-inch (10cm) swatch this way: 20 sts x 22 rows = 4 inches. To find how many *stitches* per inch that is, divide the number of stitches by the number of inches: 20 divided by 4 = 5 stitches per inch. To find how many rows per inch, divide the number of rows by the number of inches: 22 divided by 4 = 5½ rows per inch.

knit Rx

GET PLENTY OF EXERCISE!

Techie Cozy Gauge Exercise Measure the width of your cell phone (or PDA, iPod, etc.).

Multiply this number by the number of stitches per inch your chosen yarn and needles give you: this is the number of stitches you'll cast on.

Now, measure the length of your phone. Multiply this number by the number of rows per inch your chosen yarn and needles give you. Double this number: this is how many rows you'll need to knit.

Work piece until finished, bind off, fold in half length-wise and sew side seams.

Optional: Add a button and button loop with a small crocheted chain (see pages 86–87).

make-a-stitch foundation

BASIC STITCH PATTERNS

Garter Stitch

The easiest of knit stitches-and it's reversible!

Knit every stitch of every row. That's all there is to it!

Stockinette

This is the most commonly seen stitch pattern. On the public side, the individual stitches look like a series of little "v"s and on the non-public side, little bumps.

Knit all stitches in rows on the "right" or public side.

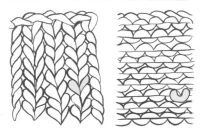

Purl all stitches in rows on the "wrong" or non-public side.

Reverse Stockinette

This is literally the opposite of stockinette stitch.

From the public side, this stitch looks like a stretchier version of garter stitch.

Purl all stitches on the "right" or public side.

Knit all stitches on the "wrong" or non-public side.

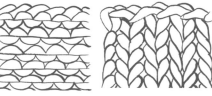

Ribbing

A great stitch that allows garments to fit well without having to do a ton of shaping—ribbing is like magic! The drawing at right is an example of k1, p1 rib (also known as 1x1 rib), but you can use any smallish number of alternating knits

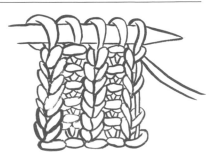

and purls to create different versions of the same effect. For maximum fabric give, use k2, p2!

(Over an *odd* number of stitches, unless it's in the round)

Row 1: *K1, p1. Repeat from * to end.

Row 2: *P1, k1. Repeat from * to end.

Continue in this manner, knitting all of the knit stitches and purling all of the purl stitches.

Seed Stitch

(Over an *even* number of stitches)

This is a lovely textured stitch achieved in the exact opposite way from k1, p1 ribbing.

Row 1:*K1, p1. *Repeat from * to end.

Row 2: *P1, k1. Repeat from * to end.

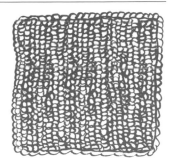

Continue in this manner, purling all of the knit stitches and knitting all of the purl stitches.

slippery when knit

THE SLIP STITCH

Use this stitch whenever you want to move a stitch without actually knitting it. It's commonly used in a variety of decreases and stitch patterns, including mosaic motifs.

1. Transfer a stitch purlwise from the left- to the right-hand needle by entering the stitch on the left-hand needle from top to bottom . . .

2. And then slipping it over. You don't actually work slipped stitches.

knit note

>> Slipping the stitch knitwise will turn the stitch so it's improperly mounted. This method is sometimes called for when you want to twist a stitch but unless specifically noted, assume that you should slip purlwise.

YO

Yarn overs are the easiest way to increase stitches, make a buttonhole, produce an eyelet, or create an airy, open-weave effect in your project.

Yarn Over Knitwise

1. Bring working yarn to the front . . .

2. And then knit stitch normally. This will wrap the yarn around the needle, creating a yarn over.

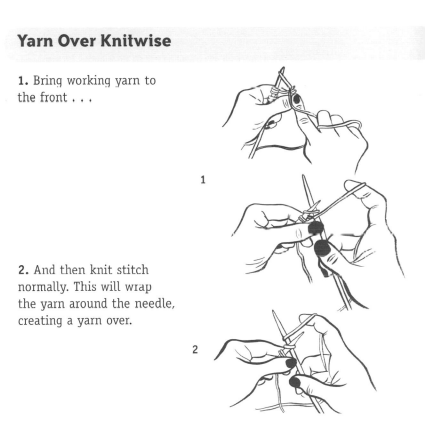

Yarn Over Purlwise

With the working yarn in front, wrap the yarn around the needle counterclockwise and purl normally.

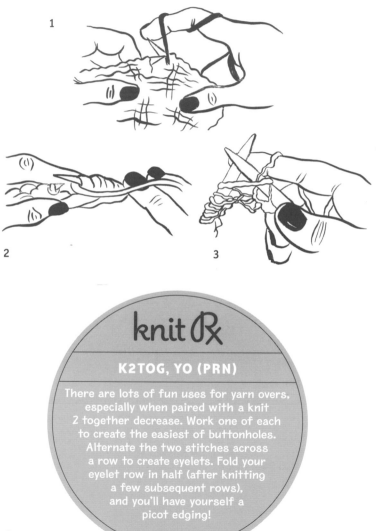

1

2   3

knit Rx

K2TOG, YO (PRN)

There are lots of fun uses for yarn overs, especially when paired with a knit 2 together decrease. Work one of each to create the easiest of buttonholes. Alternate the two stitches across a row to create eyelets. Fold your eyelet row in half (after knitting a few subsequent rows), and you'll have yourself a picot edging!

WORKING THROUGH THE BACK LOOP

Working a stitch through the back loop changes its orientation, either twisting or untwisting it depending on how it was sitting on the needle to begin with.

Knit Through the Back Loop (ktbl)

Come up through the *back* of the stitch on the left-hand needle (1) and knit as usual (see pages 33–34).

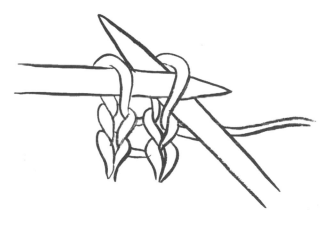

knit note

>> A knitted stitch is wider than it is tall, so there will always be more rows than stitches per inch.

Purl Through the Back Loop (ptbl)

Come down through the *back* of the stitch on the left-hand needle and purl as usual (see pages 35–36).

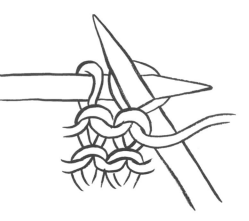

knit note

>> This is what a stitch looks like sitting on the needle the "wrong" (twisted) way.

>> This is what a stitch looks like sitting on the needle the "right" (untwisted) way.

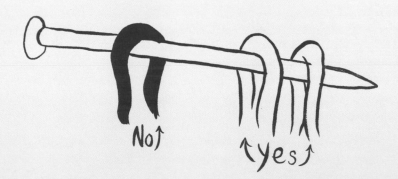

No↑   ↑yes↑

increase the piece!

INCREASE AND DECREASING

Make 1 Increase (M1)

1. With the right-hand needle, pick up loop at the base of the next stitch on the left-hand needle.

2. Place the loop on the left hand needle. Treat the loop as a new stitch and knit normally.

1

knit R_x

PREVENT ACCIDENTS

It's easy to mistake the bottom of the first stitch in a row for two stitches, causing an accidental increase. To prevent this, be sure that the working yarn is pulled down towards you when you begin a row, so that the top of the stitch will be more visible!

Knit Front and Back (K F&B) Increase

1. Knit into the front of the stitch without slipping it off the left-hand needle.

2. Knit into the back of that same stitch . . .

3. This time pulling the stitch off the needle as usual.

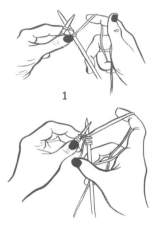

1

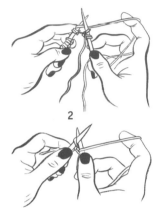

2

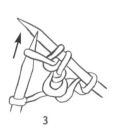

3

Purl Front and Back (PF&B) Increase

1. Purl into the front of the stitch without slipping it off the left-hand needle.

2. Purl into the back of that same stitch by coming around the back leg of the stitch and through the loop on the needle.

3. Finish as usual, pulling the stitch off the needle.

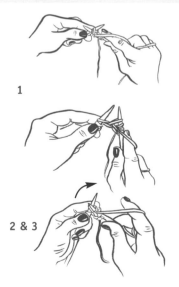

1

2 & 3

Lifted Increase

1. Lift the strand of yarn between the stitch you've just knit and the stitch that you're about to knit . . .

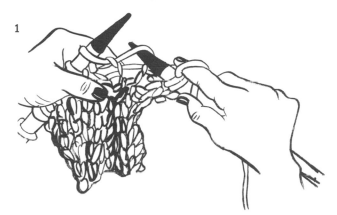

2. Placing it on the left-hand needle. Treat this as a new stitch and knit normally.

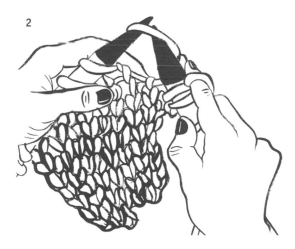

Slip Slip Knit Decrease (ssk)

1. To achieve this left-slanting decrease, slip two stitches one at a time knitwise onto the right-hand needle.

2. Knit both stitches together through the back loop.

Left-Slanting Decrease (K2togtbl)

1. Insert the needle through the *back* of two stitches on the left-hand needle.

2. Knit those two stitches together.

knit note

>> In case you're wondering why the heck it matters which type of decrease you use in a pattern, it's because the slant determines the shape of the curve you're forming, which is important for the garment's fit.

Knit Two Together (K2tog)

For this right-slanting decrease, insert the right-hand needle into the next two stitches, knitwise. Treating both stitches as one, work the knit stitch as you would normally.

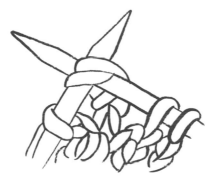

Knit Three Together (K3tog)

Super-size the K2tog by making it a right-slanting, DOUBLE DECREASE!

1. Insert the right-hand needle into the next 3 stitches, knitwise.

2. Knit all 3 stitches together.

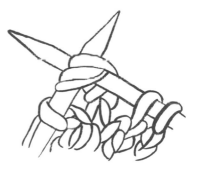

knit note

>> Pssst!!! These same decreases can be used with the purl stitch. To P2tog or P3tog, just substitute purling for the knitting! For a purl refresher, see pages 35–36.

the long and the short of knit

SHORT ROWS

Short rows create shaping by adding partial rows without casting on or off any stitches. They can be used to create bust allowance, tailored waists, sock heels or even asymmetrical stripes. For me, this little technique represents a doorway from beginning to intermediate knitting—not because it's difficult to do (no worries, Knitties, it's totally not!), but because it opens up a whole new world of almost sculptural possibilities with your needles.

You can achieve short rows in several ways, but in the interest of keeping this book pocket-sized, I'll just show you one of my faves.

Wrap-and-turn Method

Assuming you're working in stockinette stitch, knit as many stitches as required before the turning point.

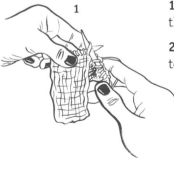

1. Slip the next stitch purlwise onto the right-hand needle . . .

2. And then bring the working yarn to the front.

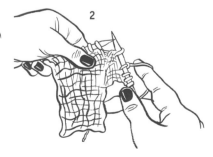

3. Slip the stitch back onto the left-hand needle, and then bring the working yarn to the back. This creates a wrapped stitch that will help prevent holes in your project.

4. Turn your work so the "wrong" (non-public) side is facing. The working yarn should already be in position to purl, so work stitches until the next desired turning point.

5. Slip the next stitch and bring the working yarn to the back.

6. Then, slip the stitch back onto the left-hand needle and return the yarn to the front. This creates the purl-side wrapped stitch. Turn your work and proceed as the pattern directs.

knit Rx

COME UNWRAPPED

To hide the wraps created by this short row method, simply work them together with the wrapped stitch when you come to them again. On a knit side, come up with your needle through the wrap AND through the wrapped stitch itself. Knit them together. On a purl side, use the tip of the right-hand needle to pick up the wrap (from the base of the back of the stitch) and place it on the left-hand needle. Purl the two stitches together.

making the rounds

KNITTING IN THE ROUND AND CINCHING OFF HATS

Joining the Round on Circulars (circs)

1. Once you've cast on the appropriate number of stitches, join the round by holding the needle end with the working yarn in your right hand and the other end in your left. Knit one stitch.

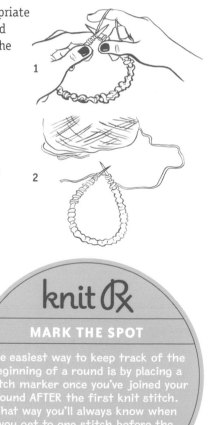

2. Then lay your circular needle down on a flat surface and make sure the stitches aren't twisted. If you can run your finger all the way around the inner part of the circle only touching the bottom part of the stitches (not the loop part), then you're good to go.

Continue knitting the round. If you find the stitches are in fact twisted, undo the stitches you've just knit, straighten out the stitches with your fingers and try again.

knit Rx

MARK THE SPOT

The easiest way to keep track of the beginning of a round is by placing a stitch marker once you've joined your round AFTER the first knit stitch. That way you'll always know when you get to one stitch before the marker, that you're ready to start your next round!

Using Circs

There's really nothing to knitting in the round with circulars. In fact, a lot of knitters prefer knitting in the round because as long as you're working in stockinette stitch, all you have to do it knit (the same by the way, goes for double pointed needles). This means no purling, because, when working in the round, you're never working on the non-public side of your project.

For me, projects in the round seem to go faster—probably because there's no stopping and starting as when you're knitting flat. It's easier for me to get into my knitting groove, ya know?

knit $\cancel{R}$

REDUCE STRESS!

Circular needles are good for more than just knitting in the round. They're a great option for knitting flat pieces, especially larger projects like blankets and adult sweaters. Circulars are less cumbersome than straight needles and the cord allows your lap to bear the weight of your knitting, rather than your wrists. Less strain on your joints means less pain. Less pain, means more knitting!

KNIT AID TO THE RESCUE

FIXING OVER-COILED CORDS Sometimes the cords on circular needles can become twisted and unruly, making them utterly impossible to work with. To tame your rogue circs, heat up a pot of water on the stove. Once the water's hot, drop your needle into the pot for 10 or so seconds. Using a pair of tongs, remove the needle from the pot. It should be unkinked by now but if not, repeat the process.

Joining Rounds on Double-Pointed Needles (dpns)

1. Once you've cast on the required number of stitches and evenly dispersed them over four needles, lay them down on a flat surface forming a square. Make sure that the stitches aren't twisted; all of the loops should be on the outer edge of your square. The needles can now be numbered 1, 2, 3, and 4 starting with the one FURTHEST away from the working yarn.

2. Once you've checked this, you're ready to join the round by introducing your last (5th) needle. To do this, hold your square in your left hand with needle #4 on the right side. Insert needle #5 into the first stitch on needle #1 . . .

3. And then knit it using the working yarn from #4.

Once you've knit that first stitch, your round is joined. At this point you can knit your round according to the pattern.

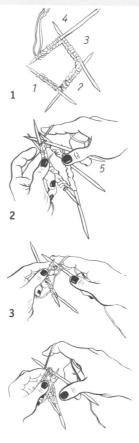

knit note

>> Although sometimes a particular pattern calls for the use of five double pointed needles, you can easily adapt it to four. If you're more comfortable using fewer needles, by all means go for it! Just read the pattern through before you start to be sure there isn't a specific reason for the recommended number of needles.

Using DPNS

Knitting with double-pointed needles can be a little intimidating, but if you keep in mind that you're only using two of the needles at any given time, it makes the process less scary. Here goes:

1. Once you've joined your round, place a marker and knit (or work whatever stitch is called for in the pattern) all the way across needle #1.

2. The needle in your left hand will now be empty. Switch the empty needle to your right hand . . .

3. And then begin knitting the stitches on needle #2.

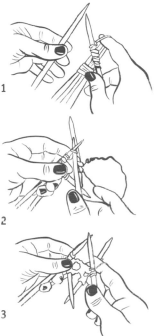

1

2

3

knit ℞

STAY GROUNDED!

If you find yourself getting frustrated with your knitting, don't be afraid to STEP AWAY FROM THE NEEDLES. I'm always "grounding" my projects until I'm in a better mood and can re-approach them with a clear head and less trucker-like cursing.

Continue in this manner until you've knitted the stitches from all the needles. You'll know that you've come to the end of the round when you come to the stitch before your marker. It's as easy as that. Knitting on dpns is awesome, people, I promise!

Cinching off a Hat

When a project like a hat has been knitted in the round and the crown shaped by decreasing, the last step is to cinch it off. Here's how it's done:

1. Cut the working yarn, leaving a 6 inch tail. Thread the tail through the tapestry needle. Run the tapestry needle through the live stitches . . .

2. Letting them slide from the knitting needle(s) onto the tail yarn. Continue in this manner until all stitches have dropped from the needle(s) onto the yarn.

3. Pull the yarn snugly until the hole is completely closed. Push the tapestry needle through to the inside of the hat. Weave in the end.

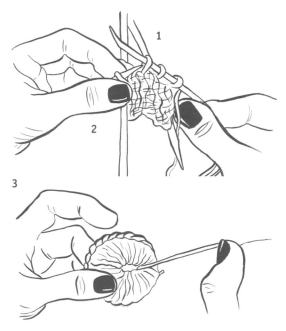

binding off
(a.k.a. casting off)

B inding off is pretty straightforward and in my humble opinion, WAY easier than its casting-on counterpart. For the most part, bind off methods are the same with only the slightest of variations depending on stitch pattern or purpose.

Basic Bind Off

1. Knit two stitches.

2. *With the tip of your left-hand needle, pull the second stitch on the right-hand needle over the first . . .

3. And then let it drop off (you'll now have one stitch left on needle).* Knit another stitch and repeat from * to ^.

Continue in this manner until all stitches are bound off.

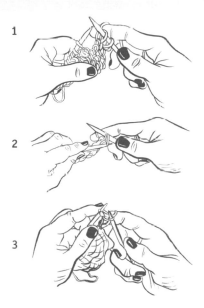

knit note

>> LAST STITCH EFFORT You'll always have one stitch left on the needle when you're done binding off. To finish the job, just cut the working yarn and pass the tail through the stitch and pull tight.

Binding Off in Ribbing

Sometimes a pattern will call for binding off in whatever pattern stitch you've been working. All this means is instead of knitting every stitch as in the basic bind off, you'll continue working in the established pattern stitch before the stitch is dropped off the needle. For example, here's how you'd bind off in Ribbing:

1. Knit one stitch, purl one stitch.

2. *With the tip of your left-hand needle, pull the second stitch on the right-hand needle over the first . . .

3. And then let it drop off (you'll now have one stitch left on needle)

4. Knit one stitch, repeat from *.

5. Purl one stitch, repeat from *.

Continue in this manner, knitting all knit stitches and purling all purled stitches until all stitches are bound off.

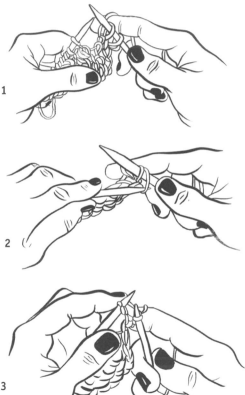

Three-Needle Bind-Off

This method is used for extra-strong seaming, for two knitted pieces with "live" stitches.

1. With the pieces still on their respective needles, place them together with right sides facing and needles parallel to each other. Bind off the two pieces at the same time as follows:

2. *Knit the first stitch on each needle together by coming up through both stitches knitwise . . .

3. And then continuing as you would if you were working with only one stitch . . . except of course, slipping BOTH stitches off of the left-hand needles.

4. You'll now have ONE stitch on the right-hand needle. Repeat from * so that you'll have two stitches on the right-hand needle.

Continue from Step 2 on basic Binding Off (see page 59).

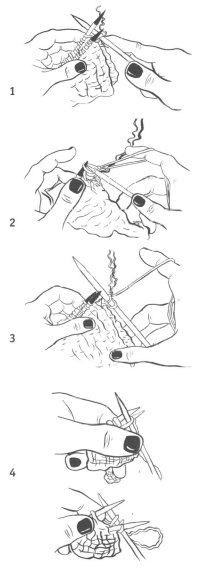

1

2

3

4

buttonholes

Like their partners in buttoning crime, buttonholes range in size from a smaller, yarn over version to a more versatile cast-on/bind-off version. Choose a button you like, then give one of these a try!

Yarn Over Version

Work stitches to the place where the buttonhole is desired.

1. Yarn over (see page 43).

2. Then knit 2 together (see page 51).

3. Continue knitting. That's all there is to it!

Horizontal Version

Row 1: Work stitches to the place where the buttonhole is desired, then bind off (see pages 59–61) the number of stitches directed by the pattern or necessary to form a hole a bit smaller than the width of the button. Continue working the row as established in the pattern.

Row 2: Work back to the gap created by the bound-off stitches. Cast on (using cable cast-on, see page 31) the same number of stitches you bound off in the previous row. Continue working row as established in pattern.

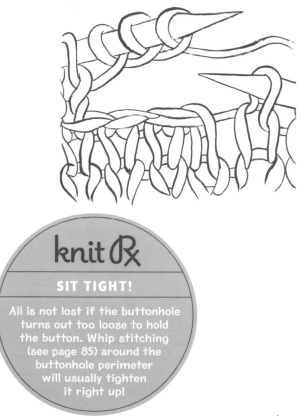

knit ℞

SIT TIGHT!

All is not lost if the buttonhole turns out too loose to hold the button. Whip stitching (see page 85) around the buttonhole perimeter will usually tighten it right up!

weaving in ends

Weaving in ends is the beginning of the finishing process. It's not only important for giving your project a polished look, but also essential for securing loose ends so that all of your hard work doesn't unravel!

Post Knitting Weave-in

Using a tapestry needle, weave loose ends in and out of stitches on wrong or "non-public" side of work. Whenever possible, weave in ends along seam lines to avoid distorting your knitted piece.

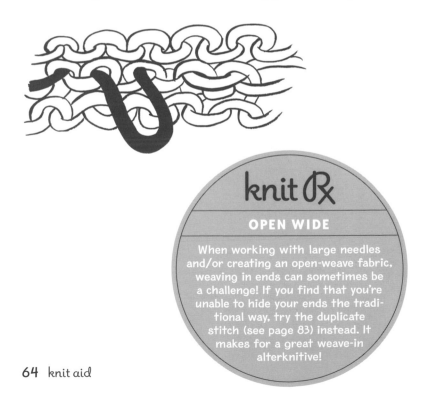

knit Rx

OPEN WIDE

When working with large needles and/or creating an open-weave fabric, weaving in ends can sometimes be a challenge! If you find that you're unable to hide your ends the traditional way, try the duplicate stitch (see page 83) instead. It makes for a great weave-in alterknitive!

WEAVING ENDS IN AS YOU KNIT

I f you're like me, you may particularly dread certain parts of the finishing process like weaving in ends. Well, if you enjoy the knitting (and who doesn't, really?) then this method will take the woe out of weaving!

English Method (Working yarn in right hand)

1. Using your left hand, hold the tail from the old yarn behind your work (right behind the row of stitches about to be knitted.

2. While you're knitting the next stitch, insert the needle under the tail. Knit the next stitch as usual.

3. Repeat those two stitches several times, until end is secure. Snip off any excess yarn.

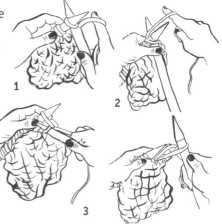

Continental Method (Working yarn in left hand)

1. Insert right hand needle knitwise into the next stitch. Using your right hand, wrap the tail around the needle counterclockwise.

2. Wrap working yarn counterclockwise.

3. Unwrap the tail from the needle (this will cause the tail and working yarn to twist), and knit the stitch as usual. Repeat until the end is secure. Snip off excess yarn.

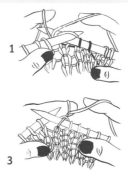

blocking

O nce you're finished with the knitting portion of your adventure, your project may need a little help in the shaping department. This is where blocking comes into play.

To block, lay out your piece(s) on an ironing board, carpeted floor, or even a table with several layers of towels taped to it (basically, you just need a flat surface that can handle a little moisture and some sewing pins). Arrange the piece(s) smoothly in the size and shape called for in the pattern's schematic. Carefully pin into place.

Using Mist and Using Steam (2)

For both methods, let dry overnight.

USING MIST Using a spray bottle on the "mist" setting, dampen piece(s).

USING STEAM
Moving an iron slowly about 4-6 inches above your project, use the steam setting to dampen piece(s). DO NOT PLACE IRON DIRECTLY ON KNITTED FABRIC.

knit ℞

TLC: CARING FOR MIXED YARN PROJECTS

Using multiple types of yarn in the same project and don't know how to care for it once it's done? No problem! As long as you wash your item according to the label of the most delicate of the yarns used, you'll be golden!

special drops

FIXING DROPPED STITCHES

Dropped Stitches (one row down)

If you drop a stitch only one row, it's not necessary to use a crochet hook to fix it. Dropped stitches look like rungs on a ladder.

1. Use the right-hand needle to pick up the loop of the stitch in the row below.

2. Place it on the left-hand needle.

3. Pull the "rung" or strand of yarn from the current row through the stitch on the needle, letting the other strand drop down over it. This loop you've just created is now the actual stitch from your current row. Knit as usual.

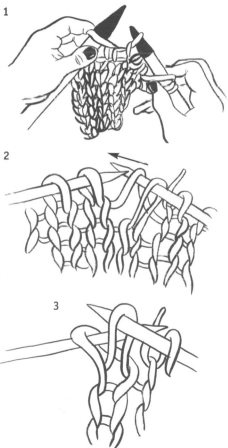

Dropped Stitches (two to five rows down)

For stitches dropped anywhere from two to five rows down, you'll want to use a crochet hook to pick them up.

1. Slip the crochet hook through the loop of the stitch that's off the needle and under the "rung" or strand of yarn closest to the stitch.

2. Pull that strand through the loop.

3. Repeat this step for as many times as rows have been dropped. Place stitch onto the left-hand needle.

Knit as usual.

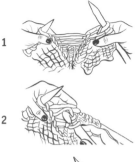

1

2

3

knit ℞

KNIT, DROP, AND ROLL!

Stockinette stitch goes from plain Jane to punk rock when purposely dropped stitches are added to an otherwise traditional-looking pattern! There are a bunch of cool patterns out there that incorporate this technique, but if you want to design your own piece (or just transform an existing pattern), it's easy to do!

I recommend twisting the stitch (ktbl) before and after the stitch you're planning on dropping—this will add a little extra stability to your piece. Assuming that you're working in stockinette stitch, you'll only need to do this on the KNIT side rows. Once you get to the place in your project where you want to start from the drop, let the intended stitch fall off of your needle and gently tug on the knitted fabric until the "ladder" reaches the bottom edge. Don't forget, though, if size matters, make sure to swatch first! Depending on the weight of yarn, dropped stitches can add inches of width to a project. Have fun!

knitional guard

HELP WITH MISTAKES

Frogging

Frogging is the process of unraveling your work when you either don't like how your project's turning out or there's a mistake too many rows down to fix. Depending on how you look at it, this is either devastating or liberating. Since I'm in a "glass full" kinda mood, let's go with the latter choice.

1. To set your yarn free from its knitted prison, just pull the knitting needle out of the stitches and set it aside.

2. Then, pull on the working yarn until you've frogged (unraveled) as much of your work as necessary. You'll be all right. I have faith in you.

knit ℞

USE A NEEDLE

If you're not completely frogging your project and only want to undo a few inches, it's helpful to stick a needle through the row of stitches where you want to stop. That way, you won't accidentally pull out too much and you'll have fewer problems locating your stitches once you're ready to start knitting again.

Unknitting

Unknitting is the best option for fixing a mistake that's anywhere from a single stitch to a couple of rows back.

1. Insert the needle in your left hand into the stitch one row below the stitch on the right-hand needle.

2. Pull slowly until the stitch on the needle comes off. Slightly tug on the working yarn to undo the stitch.

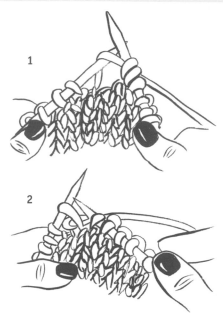

knit℞

TAKE DEEP BREATHS

Don't let your project stress you out. Remember, you're not curing disease here— it's only knitting! Mistakes can almost always either be fixed, or even better, incorporated as your very own personal design feature.

chart attack!

READING CHARTS

Charts are used any time there's a motif to be knitted into your piece, whether it's a stitch pattern or a color work design.

To read a chart, simply start at the bottom and follow along from right to left for public side rows and left to right for non-public side rows. That's all there is to it!

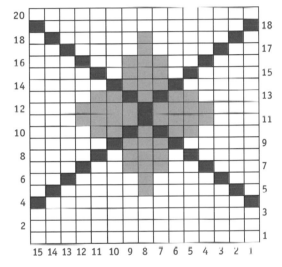

knit Rx

AVOID HEADACHES

It's often easy to lose your place in a chart, AND get a headache from trying to find it. Prevent these chart-induced side effects by using a large post-it note stuck directly beneath the working row on your chart, moving it up as you progress through the pattern. Trust me, it's really for the best.

basic cable

LEFT AND RIGHT CROSSING CABLES

Right-slanting Cable

Work several rows (according to the pattern or the distance you want your cable twists spaced apart) in stockinette stitch.

1. On a right-side row, slip half of the designated cable stitches onto a cable needle, letting that needle fall towards the BACK of the work.

2. Knit the second half of the stitches.

3. Knit the stitches off of the cable needle (you'll probably need to let the left-hand needle drop so that you can work with the cable needle for these stitches).

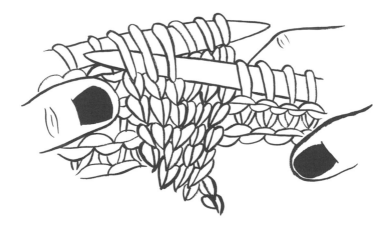

Left-slanting Cable

Work several rows (according to the pattern or the distance you want your cable twists spaced apart) in stockinette stitch.

1. On a right-side row, slip half of the designated cable stitches onto a cable needle, letting that needle fall towards the FRONT of the work.

2. Knit the second half of the stitches.

3. Knit the stitches off of the cable needle (you'll probably need to let the left-hand needle drop so that you can work with the cable needle for these stitches).

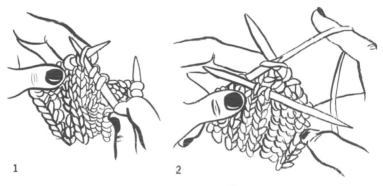

1

2

3

knitting with beads

N ow and then, I love incorporating a little bead bedazzlement into my knitting. Of course, beads can always be hand sewn onto a garment after the fact, but it's much easier to bead as you go using one of these two methods.

Pre-Stringing

First, estimate how many beads you'll need and then add a few for good measure. Choose a needle with an eye large enough to accommodate the yarn, but small enough for the bead to slide over.

1. Slide the threaded needle through the beads, one by one, until all beads are strung.

2. Knit according to pattern until one stitch before a bead is needed. Purl one stitch.

3. Slide the bead up close to the base of the stitch just purled, bring the yarn in back, and knit the next stitch.

4. Purl the next stitch. The purl stitches ensure the bead is properly mounted on the right side of the piece. Continue working as pattern directs.

Add As You Go

If you're not feeling the pre-stringing action, adding beads as you go also works!

1. Slide a bead onto a teeny crochet hook (the small ones used for doily making work best).

2. Slip the to-be-beaded stitch off of the left-hand needle and insert the crochet hook into that stitch.

3. Use your fingers to pass the bead from the hook onto the stitch. Place the stitch back onto the knitting needle, and knit the stitch as usual.

knit ℞

INTERKNIT!

Some killer, crafty Web resources for both patterns and advice!

www.vickiehowell.com
www.knitty.com
http://magknits.com/
www.yarnstandards.com
http://learntoknit.com
www.ravelry.com
http://knitting.about.com
www.interweave.com
www.stitchnbitch.org

color work

Stripes

Striping is by far the easiest and most common form of color knitting. To create a stripe, simply change to a different color of yarn at the beginning of a row. For really skinny stripes, you might change colors every other row; for thicker stripes, the sky's the limit on how often you change colors. If you choose to go the skinny route, you can usually get away with carrying the yarn along the edge of your project. This means fewer ends to weave in—YEAH! If you go for the gusto by creating wide stripes, you'll need to cut the yarn and re-join it with each color change.

SKINNY STRIPES =
2–4 rows each stripe

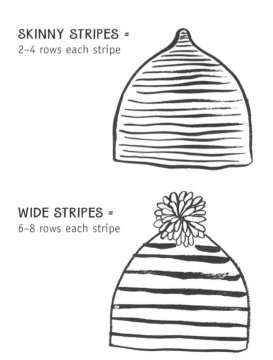

WIDE STRIPES =
6–8 rows each stripe

Fair Isle (using stranded method)

Fair Isle is a method of knitting that uses two or three different colors in the same row of your project. Instead of joining in a new ball of yarn every time the chart calls for a different color, you'll loosely carry the "inactive" color along the back or "non-public" side of the work.

The easiest way to do this is:

1. To hold one color in each hand (dropping and picking up a third color, if called for) . . .

2. And knitting with both.

In other words, you'll be using both the English AND the Continental methods to knit, alternating method's depending on which hand's yarn is called for. I recommend laying your project flat every once in awhile, to make sure that no puckering has occurred.

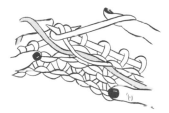

1 Working on public side.

Working on non-public side.

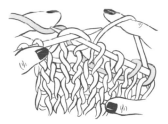

2 Working on public side.

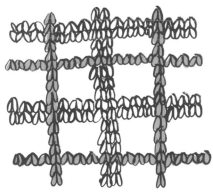

This is what Fair Isle knitting looks like.

Intarsia

Intarsia is a method of knitting that involves color blocks. Following a chart, you'll literally knit a simple picture into your garment.

Work in the main color, switching to the pattern color(s) as called for by the design.

1. For each section of color, you should use a separate ball (or bobbin) of yarn to avoid fabric puckering.

2. When changing from one ball of yarn to another, make sure to wrap around or over the neighboring yarn to avoid holes. Don't worry if your garment doesn't seem to be lying perfectly flat as you're knitting. With intarsia projects, blocking almost always fixes any misshaping that occurs.

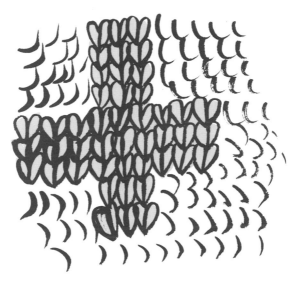

This is what Intarsia knitting looks like.

Mosaic Knitting

Mosaic knitting is, in my humble opinion, among the most user-friendly of color work options. There's no carrying of multiple yarns across your rows and no worry of holes being created by changing yarns between color blocks. Mosaic knitting involves two different colors of yarn, only one of which is actually used to knit in any given row. You only change yarn at the beginning of every other row, as if you were knitting 2-row stripes.

1. Following a chart and starting on the public side of your project, knit with the designated color while slipping the stitches of the second color purlwise.

2. Repeat this process on the non-public side. Reverse the process for the next two rows, working only the stitches you slipped on the previous two rows.

3. Continue as established, following chart and switching working yarn every other row until pattern is finished.

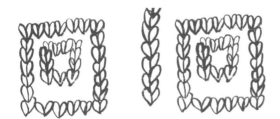

This is what mosaic knitting looks like.

knit note

>> Always cast on with the color of yarn OPPOSITE of what you're going to knit for your first row of stitches. Oh, and to determine which color you begin knitting with, just look at the first square in the right-hand corner of the chart!

hey there, how ya felting?

FELTING

Hand Felting

Hand felting works great for small projects! Fill a large bowl with hottish water (making it no warmer than your hands can comfortably handle) and about a tablespoon of gentle soap. Lots of soaps out there are made especially for felting, but I've found that shampoo works just fine. After all, if it's gentle enough for my overly-processed hair, then it's gentle enough for yarn!

1. The key to felting is agitation, so after placing your project into the soapy water . . .

2. Vigorously scrunch and rub the wool piece against itself.

3. After a couple of minutes, stop to check out your work. If you're satisfied with how it looks, then rinse the piece out with cool water.

If you're feeling like your project isn't felt-y enough yet, then repeat the process until you're satisfied. Remember, the longer the project stays moving in the water solution, the less stitch definition will remain!

Machine Felting

1. Place the knitted project in a zippered pillowcase or fine mesh bag.

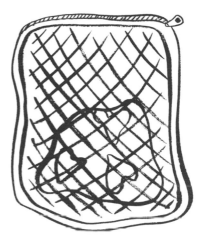

2. Throw the bag into the washing machine along with an old pair of jeans or towel (this will help with agitation) and wash with hot water, omitting the "spin" portion of the washing cycle. Repeat as many times as necessary to achieve the desired result. Take care to check on your project every five minutes or so.

3. When finished, squeeze out excess water (rolling in a towel works well) . . .

4. And shape per pattern instructions, letting dry on a towel. Remember that felting works only with natural animal fibers that have not been "superwash" treated.

knit note

>> **Keep in mind that there is no science to felting. Even though you can count on about 30 percent vertical shrinkage, your mileage may vary. If there ever was a time to swatch, this is it!**

embroidery and finishing stitches

Mattress Stitch

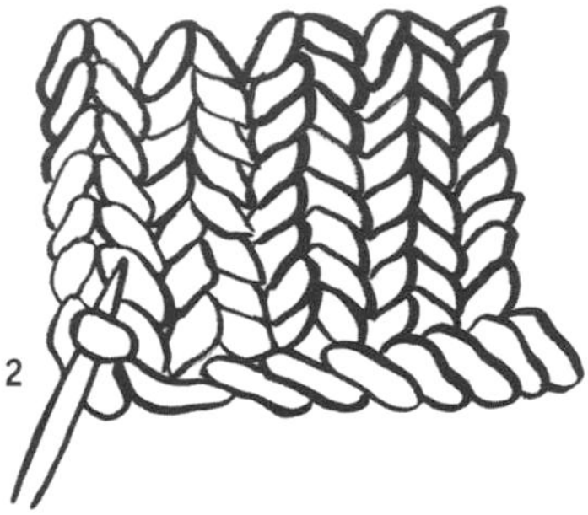

1. Lay the two knitted pieces that you want to seam side by side, with the right sides facing you. If you gently pull the edge stitch away from the stitch next to it, you'll notice a row of bars between the stitches.

1 & 2

2. Come up through the back edge of one of your pieces with a tapestry needle and yarn, insert the needle under one of the bars . . .

3

3. And then pull the yarn through. Repeat this step on your second piece.

4. Continue picking up bars. You'll notice your edges slowly beginning to fold inward, creating an almost seamless seam! Continue in this manner until finished. Securely weave in the ends.

Duplicate Stitch

1. Using a tapestry needle and yarn of the same weight or a slightly finer weight than that of your project, come up through the bottom of the "V" of the knit stitch.

2. Insert the needle under both loops of the stitch above the one you're duplicating . . .

3. And, pull the yarn through, and go back down through the point of the "V" where you started.

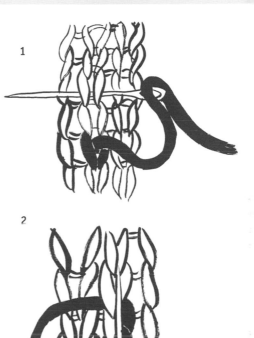

Kitchener Stitch

Kitchener stitch is a magically delicious way of seamlessly joining two pieces of knitted fabric, using "live" stitches. This stitch is most commonly used to graft toes in sock patterns.

1. Place an equal number of stitches on two needles. Hold the needles in one hand, parallel to each other with wrong sides of the knitting facing. A length of the working yarn, cut when you finished your knitting, should be conveniently hanging from the back needle to begin your seam.

2. Using your other hand, insert the tapestry needle through the first stitch on the FRONT needle purlwise, leaving it on the needle.

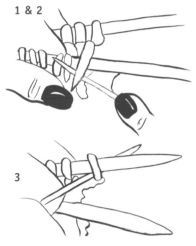

3. Then, come through the first stitch on the BACK needle knitwise, also leaving it on the needle. Draw the yarn through. These steps have created a stable start.

4. *Come through the first stitch on the FRONT needle knitwise, letting it drop off the needle.

5. Come through the next stitch on the FRONT needle purlwise, leaving it on the needle.

6. Come through the first stitch on the BACK needle purlwise, letting it fall off the needle.

7. Come through the next stitch on the BACK needle knitwise, leaving it on the needle. Draw the yarn through.

Repeat from * until finished, stopping every few stitches to ensure the grafting is going smoothly.

Whip Stitch

The most basic of sewing stitches, the whip stitch is most commonly used to baste or finish an area that will not be seen. Although I don't recommend this stitch for any area that will experience stress, it's easy to achieve and works well for things like hemlines.

1. With yarn and a tapestry needle, and working from back to front, come up through your piece(s).

2. Go around piece edge(s) and repeat where you'd like your next stitch to be. The closer the repeats, the shorter the stitch length. Repeat until finished, beginning the new stitch right next to the old one.

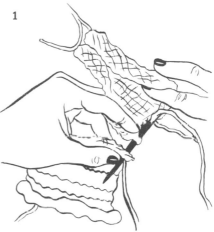

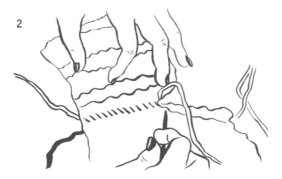

hooked on faux-knits

CROCHETED EDGINGS

Crocheted Chain (ch)

1. Tie a slipknot onto a crochet hook. This will act as your first stitch. Wrap yarn counter-clockwise around the hook . . .

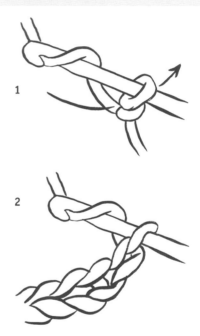

2. And pull through the stitch on the hook. Continue in this manner until your chain is the desired length.

knit note

>> It helps to hold the tail of the yarn securely between your thumb and middle finger while you're working!

Single Crochet (sc) Edging

1. Tie a slipknot onto the crochet hook. Insert hook into the front loop of the knitted edge stitch you're embellishing.

2. You now have two loops (stitches) on your hook. Wrap yarn counterclockwise around the hook and draw it through the first loop.

3. Wrap yarn once counterclockwise again, and draw through both loops.

4. *Insert hook into the next knit stitch. Wrap yarn and draw through the first loop . . .

5. And then wrap yarn again and draw it through both loops. Continue from * until the edging is complete.

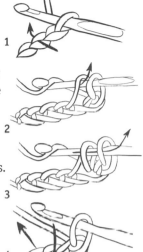

Half Double-Crochet (hdc) Edging

Following instructions above, single crochet into the first of your knitted edge stitches.

1. Wrap yarn once counterclockwise . . .

2. And insert hook into the next knitted stitch.

3. You now have three loops on your hook. Wrap yarn and pull through the first loop . . .

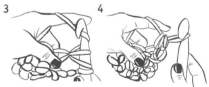

4. Then wrap again, pulling through **all three** loops. Continue in this manner until the edging is complete.

Double Crochet (dc)

Following instructions on page 87, single crochet into the first of your knitted edge stitches.

1. Wrap yarn counterclockwise around the hook once . . .

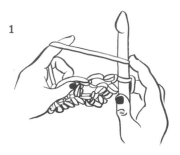

2. And insert it into BOTH LOOPS of the stitch from the row below (or the chain stitch for the first row).

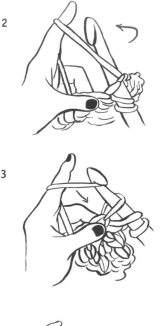

3. Wrap yarn counterclockwise around hook again and draw it through the first two loops.

4. Wrap yarn once counterclockwise again, and draw through the last two loops. Continue in this manner across the row or as the pattern suggests. Double crochet, completed, looks like this:

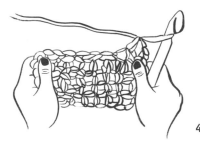

embellishments

I-Cord

1. With a double-pointed or circular needle, cast on stitches and knit across row.

2. Once that row is complete, slide the stitches to the opposite end of the needle . . .

3. And switch hands so that the needle (or end, if you're working with a circular needle) with the stitches is in your left hand. The working yarn will appear to be at the wrong end of the row . . .

4. But bring it behind the stitches and begin knitting again.

The strand of yarn stretched across the back will create a tube. Continue in this manner until your I-cord is the desired length.

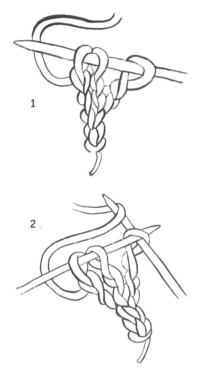

knit note

>> I-cord is awesome! Use it to make shoelaces, button loops, bootie ties, drawstrings, necklaces, and oh so much more. Use it: it's your friend.

Pom-Poms

1. Cut out two cardboard circles as big in diameter as you'd like your pom-pom to be. Working about ½ inch in from the edge, cut out the centers of each circle so the pieces look like donuts. For ease in wrapping yarn, cut both donuts from the outer edge to the center to allow you to slip the yarn into the center as you wrap.

2. Place circles together and begin wrapping yarn around the edge of the circles.

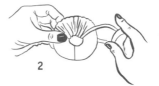

3. Continue in this manner until entire "donut" is covered once or twice over.

4. Place the blade of your scissors in between the two layers of cardboard and carefully cut the loops of yarn created by the wrap-arounds.

5. Take another piece of yarn and tie the yarn strands between the cardboard pieces together securely.

6. Remove cardboard. Fluff pom-pom and trim if necessary.

Tassels

Wrap three to five strands of yarn around a CD case (or small piece of cardboard), about 20 to 40 times (depending on weight of yarn). Carefully slide yarn off the case and pinch together about an inch down from one end, cinching tightly, using an additional strand of yarn. Cut loops at the opposite end, creating tassel strands.

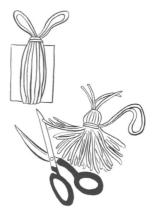

Fringe

Cut three to five strands (depending on how thick you'd like your fringe) of yarn **double** the length of your desired finished embellishment.

1. Holding strands together, fold in half.

2. Insert a crochet hook (any size) through the right side of the edge of your project and lay yarn at the folded point over the hook.

3. Pull the yarn through, from back to front, just enough to create a loop.

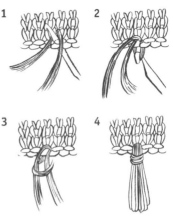

4. Set aside the crochet hook and use your hands to fold the loop over the edge of the project, and pull the ends of the yarn through the loop. Pull tight.

Needle Felting

1. Place a two-inch foam block inside of project, directly under the spot you want to embellish. Lay out your stencil(s) and once you're satisfied with their placement, use a size 38 felting needle to lightly stab a small amount of roving into place.

2. Slowly add more roving, making sure the fiber is situated exactly where you'd like it. Stab roving repeatedly, permanently attaching it to the project. Repeat the process until the design is complete.

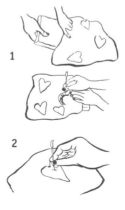

s*t*a*s*h 4077

USING YOUR STASH

Whether you're a yarn hoarder (not that there's anything wrong with that) or a better-safe-than-sorry over-buyer, chances are that if you knit then you also have a yarn stash. Hey, I'm all about surrounding myself with as much fiber-y delight as possible!

There comes a time my friend, however, when one must deplete one's collection in order to make room for restocking. Here are my top ten suggestions for stash-friendly projects, most with patterns that are only an internet search away!

1. Felted potholders or coasters (great for chunky yarns!)

2. Striped kids' sweater (pick several yarns in the same weight and substitute "stash stripes" for the yarn called for in any basic pattern)

3. Baby booties or mittens (leftover sock yarn is perfect for these!)

4. Baby hat (almost any weight of yarn works!)

5. Feather and Fan Scrap Shawl (see page 93 for pattern)

6. Stitch Sample Throw (a bunch of squares sewn together, knitted in as many different yarns as you'd like, makes for a snuggly, tangible record of your mad stitch pattern skillz!)

7. Camera, cell phone or iPod cozy (see page 39 for pattern suggestions)

8. Washcloths (Use cotton blend yarns and pair with organic soaps for a gift anyone would love!)

9. Wristbands and wristwarmers (fashionable *and* functional)

10. Knitted embellishments (add knitted flowers, edgings, or ruffles to pre-made pillowcases, purses, and clothing)

GREEN PIECE

YARN ALTERNATIVES Years ago, those who preferred not to work with animal fibers such as wool, cashmere, and alpaca due to allergies or social consciousness had very limited choices: acrylic, cotton, or nylon blends. Thanks to modern technology, however, this is no longer the case! Exciting new fibers are available from bamboo and soy to banana leaves and corn.

Experimenting with different yarns is half the fun of knitting. After all, the same project can have a completely different outcome depending on your choice of fiber.

STASH WRAP

FEATHER AND FAN WRAP MADE FROM SCRAPS FROM YOUR STASH!

MATERIALS

Several balls of different bulky weight yarns (or lighter weight yarns, double-stranded) in desired color scheme.

US size 17 (12.75mm) needles

Tapestry needle

DIRECTIONS

Using first color, CO 56 sts. *Work 4-row pattern. Switch to next yarn choice, repeat 4-row pattern. Continue in this manner, switching yarns for each pattern repeat, until piece measures 72 inches (or desired length). BO. Weave in ends.

STITCH PATTERN

Multiple of 18 + 2

Row 1 (RS): Knit.

Row 2: Purl.

Row 3: K1, *K2tog 3 times, (YO, K1) 6 times, K2tog 3 times; rep from * to last st, K1.

Row 4: Knit.

Repeat these 4 rows.

(Source: *365 Knitting Stitches A Year: Perpetual Calendar,* Martingale & Company, 2002).

△*t*α*△*h 40TT 93

Acknowledgments

First off, to all of you who've suffered through my shamelessly bad puns and ridiculous dedication to theme, I thank you. If you also happened to laugh out loud at my attempts at wit, then I thank you even more. I've always thought writing comedy, or perhaps, even doing stand-up comedy would be fun. Well, except for the part when the audience "boos," or even worse, does nothing. There's nothing worse than the sound of crickets chirping indoors. Actually, instead of a back-up career in comedy, I think I'd prefer to start my own pun writing company. I'd call it something catchy like The Pundits or The Punishers. I would single-handedly cheapen products, current events, and companies by making them punbelievable! Ohhh, those would be good times. Good times. But I digress.

First and foremost, I owe huge amounts of gratitude to the gang at **Sterling Publishing**, especially **Steve Magnussen** for listening to my on-the-fly pitch; my editor and fellow Irish-broad-in-crime, **Jo Fagan**; the beautiful and talented publicity maven, **Leigh Ann Ambrosi**; **Krista Margies**, publicist extraordinaire; and editor, **Rodman Neumann**, whose patience and attention to detail blows my mind. I feel so lucky to be working with such an amazing group of people! And I'd like to thank **Leela Corman** for her incredible art.

As always, I'd like to extend tons of thanks and gooshy-mushiness to the **Knitty Gritty** producers and crew, as well as to everyone at **DIY Network**. I really appreciate your support—especially when it comes in the form of cocktails. I kid! I joke!

This book was written over the course of a month which would have been utterly impossible without the love, understanding, and help managing Kidsville USA '06 (a.k.a. my household) from my handsome sweetheart of a man, **Dave Campbell**. Thank you to my beautiful boys: **Tanner**, who is going through an "anti-kissing" stage, and **Tristan**, who seems to be prepping for careers in both music and politics—for constantly entertaining me with your hilarious antics. I love you "to a hundred and all the numbers that nobody can count to!" To the two most influential women in my life, my best friend **Tammy Izbicki**, and my mom, **Libby Bailey**: you've taught me the meaning of having a village. You are my She-everythings. Lastly, I'd like to give a special shout out to **Adina Klein**, **Mike Faulkner**, **Jenny Medford**, **Kevin Iudicello**, **Jennifer Perkins**, **Steve Bae**, **Kelly Mooney**, and the **Meowers** for your advice, comedy-filled posts and instant messages, constant friendship, and invaluable support. I ♥ you all!

Index

About the Author

A self-proclaimed crafty gRRRL, **Vickie Howell** has been involved in the creative arts for as long as she can remember. Before becoming the mother of two boys, she worked in the entertainment industry at companies including International Creative Management (ICM) and Alliance Atlantis Entertainment. Post-motherhood, she has founded three crafty Web-based businesses and two Stitch 'n Bitch groups. She is the host of HGTV & DIY television's *Knitty Gritty*, co-host of *Stylelicious*, and a founding member of the infamous Austin Craft Mafia. She writes regular columns for both Vogue's *Knit.1* and *KIWI* magazines and has a line of luxurious eco-friendly yarn, The Vickie Howell Collection, with renowned fiber company, SWTC. More of

her designs can be found in her Sterling Publishing Co. books *New Knits on the Block* and *Not Another Teen Knitting Book*, as well as her Web site and a variety of other publications nationwide. Vickie lives, breathes, and knits in Austin, Texas. For more info, check out www.vickiehowell.com

10% of the royalties from this book will go to aid victims of disaster. Visit www.redcross.org for more info on how you can help.